Uncle Ben's Instant Clip-Quotes

Benjamin R. De Jong

BAKER BOOK HOUSE
Grand Rapids, Michigan 49506

Contents

Advice   5

Ambition   23

Attitude   31

Bible   33

Challenge   39

Character   43

Christ   47

Christian   51

Church   59

Commitment   61

Consistency   63

Criticism   77

Discipline   79

Egotism   81

Faithfulness   83

God   87

Home   93

Lighter Vein   95

Love   99

Prayer   105

Service   111

Sin   113

Warning   115

Wisdom   119

Worldliness   121

Worry   125

Advice

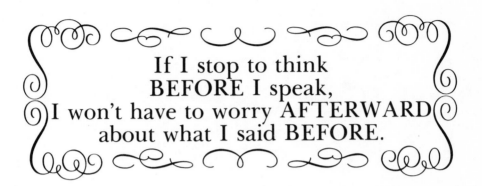

If I stop to think
BEFORE I speak,
I won't have to worry AFTERWARD
about what I said BEFORE.

Don't think people judge your generosity
by the amount of advice you give away.

If you can't make light of your
troubles, keep them in the dark.

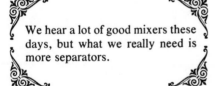

We hear a lot of good mixers these
days, but what we really need is
more separators.

Change the contents of the heart and you
will alter the droppings of the mouth.

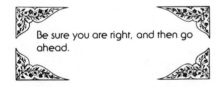

Be sure you are right, and then go
ahead.

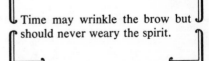

Time may wrinkle the brow but
should never weary the spirit.

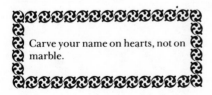

Carve your name on hearts, not on
marble.

Do unto others as though you were
the others.

If you wouldn't write it
and sign it,
don't say it.

Withdraw thy foot from thy
neighbor's house; lest he be
weary of thee, and so hate thee
(Prov. 25:17).

When we see the lilies
    spinning in distress.
Taking thought to manufacture
    their own loveliness.
When we see the birds all building
    barns for store,
'Twill then be time to worry
    —not before!

Habit is a cable;
we weave a thread of it every day,
and at last
we cannot break it.

The trouble with a lot of smart kids is
that they don't smart in the right place.

7

GIFTS
To your enemy, FORGIVENESS.
To an opponent, TOLERANCE.
To a friend, YOUR HEART.
To a customer, SERVICE.
To all men, CHARITY.
To every child, A GOOD EXAMPLE.
To yourself, RESPECT.

A continual dropping in a very rainy day and a contentious woman are the same (Prov. 27:15).

A peck of common sense is worth a bushel of learning.

BE SYMPATHETIC;
you know it could happen to you.

Work is the best thing ever invented for killing time.

9

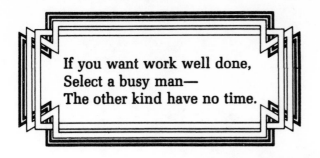

If you want work well done,
Select a busy man—
The other kind have no time.

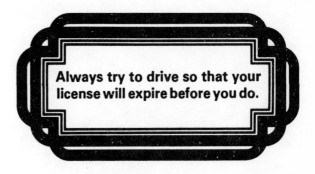

Always try to drive so that your
license will expire before you do.

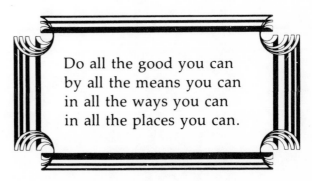

If you want the world
to HEED,
Put your CREED
Into your DEED.

Do all the good you can
by all the means you can
in all the ways you can
in all the places you can.

Itching for what you want
doesn't do much good —
you've got to scratch for it.

The secret of contentment is
knowing how to enjoy what you
have and be able to lose all desire
for things beyond your reach.

A word fitly spoken is like apples
of gold in pictures of silver
(Prov. 25:11).

Deal with the faults of others as
gently as with your own.
—Henrichs

Never throw mud.
You may not hit your mark,
but you will have
dirty hands.

Seconds count, especially when dieting.

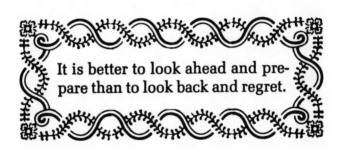

The only way to settle a disagreement
is on the basis of what's right—
not who's right.

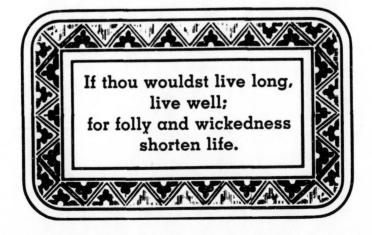

It is better to look ahead and prepare than to look back and regret.

If thou wouldst live long,
live well;
for folly and wickedness
shorten life.

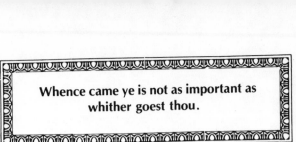

Whence came ye is not as important as whither goest thou.

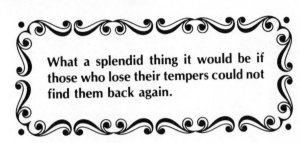

What a splendid thing it would be if those who lose their tempers could not find them back again.

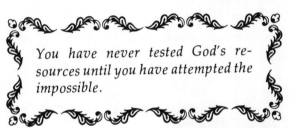

You have never tested God's resources until you have attempted the impossible.

If you think you are too small to do a big thing, try doing small things in a big way.

**OVERLOOK
the faults of others
but LOOK OVER
your own carefully.**

Folks who never do any more than they are paid for, never get paid for any more than they do.

A temper is a valuable possession, don't lose it.

It is never the right time to do the wrong thing.

A child of God should be serious without being sour, and happy without being foolish.

A good place to find a helping hand is at the end of your arm.

A soft answer has often been the means of breaking a hard heart.

A CREED FOR EVERYONE

SILENCE when your words would hurt.
PATIENCE when your neighbor's curt.
DEAFNESS when the scandal flows.
THOUGHTFULNESS for other's woes.
PROMPTNESS when stern duty calls.
COURAGE when misfortune falls.

It is not he who has little, but he who wants more, who is poor.

WAIT ON

To talk with God,
*   No breath is lost—*
Talk on!

To walk with God,
*   No strength is lost—*
Walk on!

To wait on God,
*   No time is lost—*
Wait on!

To stay youthful stay useful.

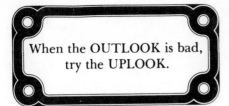
When the OUTLOOK is bad,
try the UPLOOK.

It's right to be contented with
what you have but never with
what you are.

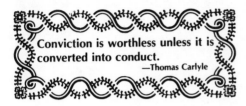
Conviction is worthless unless it is
converted into conduct.
—Thomas Carlyle

Walk softly.
Speak tenderly.
Pray fervently.

If you are planning to do a mean thing,
wait until tomorrow,
If a good thing,
do it today.

YESTERDAY is a cancelled check.
TOMORROW is a promissory note.
TODAY is the only cash you have.
Spend it wisely.

You must
LET GO
before you can
LAY HOLD.

A smile is an asset,
a frown is a liability.

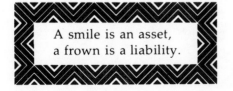

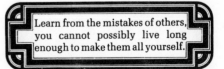
Learn from the mistakes of others,
you cannot possibly live long
enough to make them all yourself.

Ambition

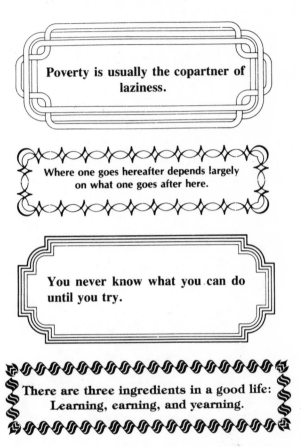

Poverty is usually the copartner of laziness.

Where one goes hereafter depends largely on what one goes after here.

You never know what you can do until you try.

There are three ingredients in a good life: Learning, earning, and yearning.

Seest thou a man diligent in business? He shall stand before kings (Prov. 22:29).

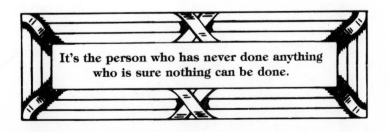

It's the person who has never done anything who is sure nothing can be done.

Jumping at conclusions is not half as good exercise as digging for the facts.

All that is necessary for the triumph of evil is that good men do nothing.

Common sense is seeing things as they are, and doing things as they should be done.

Let your aim and aspiration be not to enjoy life, but to employ it.

The measure of your usefulness is determined by the measure of your consecration.

If at first you don't succeed, try a little ARDOR.

It is a great thing to do little things well.

He becometh poor who dealeth with a slack hand; but the hand of the diligent maketh rich (Prov. 10:4).

The best way to get rid of unpleasant duties is to discharge them faithfully.

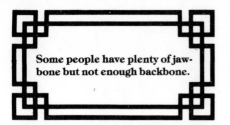
Some people have plenty of jaw-bone but not enough backbone.

What you can do,
you ought to do,
and what you
ought to do,
by the help of God
DO!

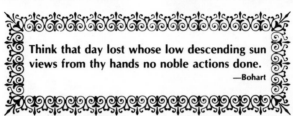
Think that day lost whose low descending sun views from thy hands no noble actions done.
—Bohart

A TRUE MINISTER
God's man in
God's place, doing
God's work, in
God's way, for
God's glory.

No life can be dreary when work is delight.

The dictionary is the only place where you will find SUCCESS before WORK.

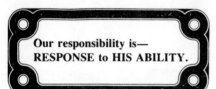
Our responsibility is—
RESPONSE to HIS ABILITY.

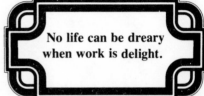
A revolving fan gathers no flies.

A smooth sea never made a skillful sailor.

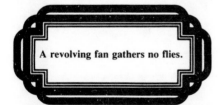
A good thing to remember,
a better thing to do—
work with the construction gang,
not with the wrecking crew.

I am not what I ought to be;
I am not what I wish to be;
But by the grace of God,
I am not what I used to be.

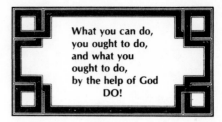

Work is the yeast that raises the dough.

The greatest
ABILITY
is
DEPENDABILITY

Spin CAREFULLY,
Not TEARFULLY,
Though WEARILY you plod.
Spin CAREFULLY,
Spin PRAYERFULLY,
But leave the thread with God.

The lazy man aims at nothing and usually hits it.

Life is like a grindstone, and whether it grinds a man down or polishes him depends on the stuff he is made of.

The man who is waiting for something to turn up might do well to start with his own shirt sleeves.

Some people take a stand for Christ, and never move again.

Little strokes fell great oaks.

No one is a failure in this world who lightens a burden for someone else.

If a man does only what is required of him,
he is a slave.
If a man does more than is required of him,
he is a free man.

Experience gained the hard way brings knowledge that remains.

What is gotten
without effort
is not worth
what it cost.

It is not so much what we know as how well we use what we know.

29

Attitude

MR. MOODY SAID:
It does not take long to tell where a man's treasure is. In fifteen minutes' conversation with most men, you can tell whether their treasures are on earth or in heaven.

A righteous man regardeth the life of his beast; but the tender mercies of the wicked are cruel (Prov. 12:10).

No one can possibly go forward in the strength of the Lord until he has first learned to stand still in his own helplessness.

He who has the most trouble usually has been busy making it.

The most important ingredient in the formula of success is knowing how to get along with people.

Nothing will cook your goose faster than a red hot temper.

A soft answer turneth away wrath; but grievous words stir up anger (Prov. 15:1).

A GRUDGE
is too heavy a load
for anyone
to carry.

Forget each kindness that you do as soon as you have done it.
Forget the praise that falls to you the moment you have won it.
Forget the slander that you hear before you can repeat it.
Forget each slight, each spite, each sneer, whenever you may meet it.
Remember every promise made and keep it to the letter.
Remember those who lend you aid and be a grateful debtor.
Remember all the happiness that comes your way in living.
Forget each worry and distress, be hopeful and forgiving.
Remember good, remember truth, remember heaven is above you.
And you will find, through age and youth, that many will love you.

Bible

Look to other books for
INFORMATION
But look only to the Bible for
TRANSFORMATION

No atheist can injure the Bible's influence so thoroughly as a Christian who disregards it in his daily life.

The Bible may cause you to wonder, but it will never cause you to wander.

Many Christians spend more time reading the newspaper than they do the Bible.

You can learn a lot from the Bible; you can learn still more practicing it.

The Bible promises no loaves for the loafer.

The Bible will not be a dry book if you know the Author.

In every step, in every stride,
I'll let the Savior be my guide!
His Word, His love, I will embrace,
And let His wisdom set the pace.

When the Bible speaks
discussion is useless;
when the Bible is silent
discussion ends.

We must feed on the Bread of Life
ourselves before we can serve it to
others.

If it is in the Bible, it is SO!

The degree of our spiritual vigor will
be in direct proportion to the time
we spend in God's Word.

THE WORD OF GOD

For feelings come and feelings go,
And feelings are deceiving;
My warrant is the Word of God
Nought else is worth believing.
I'll trust in God's unchanging Word
Till soul and body sever:
For, though all things shall pass away,
His Word shall stand forever.

Either the Bible will keep you from sin
or sin will keep you from the Bible.

Study the Bible to be wise; believe it
to be safe; practice it to be holy.

YOUR OWN VERSION
You are writing a Gospel,
A chapter each day,
By deeds that you do,
By words that you say.
Men read what you write,
Whether faithless or true;
Say, what is the Gospel
According to YOU?

The mirror of the Word is painfully
clear.

There are two parts to the Gospel:
BELIEVING IT
and
BEHAVING IT.

A knowledge of the Bible without
a college education is more valuable than a college education
without a knowledge of the Bible.

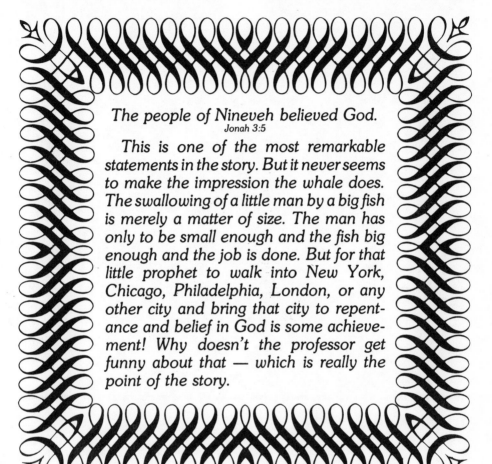

The people of Nineveh believed God.
Jonah 3:5

This is one of the most remarkable statements in the story. But it never seems to make the impression the whale does. The swallowing of a little man by a big fish is merely a matter of size. The man has only to be small enough and the fish big enough and the job is done. But for that little prophet to walk into New York, Chicago, Philadelphia, London, or any other city and bring that city to repentance and belief in God is some achievement! Why doesn't the professor get funny about that — which is really the point of the story.

Challenge

There's so much good in the worst of us,
And so much bad in the best of us,
That it's hard to tell which one of us
Ought to reform the rest of us.

FAITHFULNESS TO CHRIST—
Put DANIEL in the lion's den;
Cast his THREE FRIENDS in the furnace;
Made STEPHEN the first martyr;
Took JOHN BAPTIST'S head off;
Caused PETER to be crucified;
Brought PAUL to the execution block;
Burned EARLY CHRISTIANS at the stake.
QUESTION: What does it cost us?

The world is the better or the worse for everyone who lives in it.

What fruit have ye from the things whereof ye are now ashamed? For the end of those things is death (Rom. 6:21)

If you were another person, would you like to be a friend of yourself?

Shamgar had an OX GOAD,
David had a SLING,
Dorcas had a NEEDLE,
Rahab had some STRING,
Mary had some OINTMENT,
Moses had a ROD,
Have YOU some SMALL TALENT
You'll dedicate TO GOD?

Life is short
Death is sure
Sin the cause
Christ the cure.

A man has to live with himself, and he should see to it that he always has good company.

For every benefit you receive, a responsibility is levied.

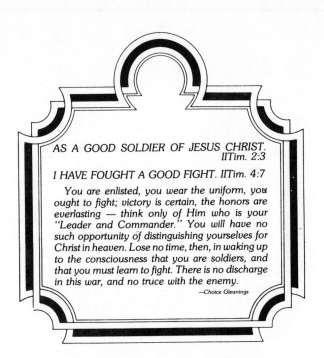

AS A GOOD SOLDIER OF JESUS CHRIST.
IITim. 2:3

I HAVE FOUGHT A GOOD FIGHT. IITim. 4:7

You are enlisted, you wear the uniform, you ought to fight; victory is certain, the honors are everlasting — think only of Him who is your "Leader and Commander." You will have no such opportunity of distinguishing yourselves for Christ in heaven. Lose no time, then, in waking up to the consciousness that you are soldiers, and that you must learn to fight. There is no discharge in this war, and no truce with the enemy.

—Choice Gleanings

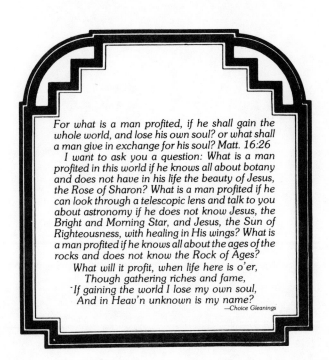

For what is a man profited, if he shall gain the whole world, and lose his own soul? or what shall a man give in exchange for his soul? Matt. 16:26

I want to ask you a question: What is a man profited in this world if he knows all about botany and does not have in his life the beauty of Jesus, the Rose of Sharon? What is a man profited if he can look through a telescopic lens and talk to you about astronomy if he does not know Jesus, the Bright and Morning Star, and Jesus, the Sun of Righteousness, with healing in His wings? What is a man profited if he knows all about the ages of the rocks and does not know the Rock of Ages?

What will it profit, when life here is o'er,
Though gathering riches and fame,
If gaining the world I lose my own soul,
And in Heav'n unknown is my name?

—Choice Gleanings

Character

Behavior is a mirror in which we show our image.

There is nothing truly great in any man—except character.

Character needs no epitaph. You can bury a man, but character will beat the hearse back from the graveyard.

The measure of a man's real character is what he would do if he knew he would never be found out.

Character is not made in a crisis—it is only exhibited.

Our true selves are usually revealed in our seemingly trivial acts.

A golden character needs no gilding.

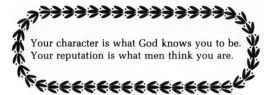
Your character is what God knows you to be.
Your reputation is what men think you are.

A beautiful heart
seems to transform
the homeliest face.

It is HUMAN
to stand with the
CROWD.
It is DIVINE
to stand
ALONE.

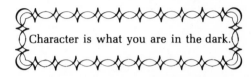
Character is what you are in the dark.

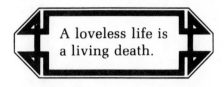
A loveless life is
a living death.

A bad conscience
has a good memory.

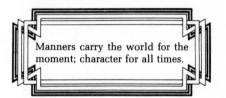
Manners carry the world for the
moment; character for all times.

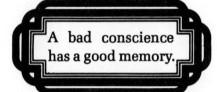
'Tis beauty that doth oft make women proud;
'Tis virtue that doth make them most admired;
'Tis modesty that makes them seem divine.

What you possess in this world
will go to someone else when you
die, but what you are will be yours
forever.

Fads come and go; common sense
goes on forever.

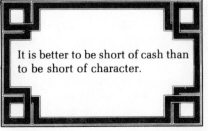
It is better to be short of cash than
to be short of character.

What you laugh at tells plainer
than words what you are.

45

Christus

Christ is our Peace; the sins of YESTERDAY
By His most precious blood are washed away.
Christ is our Life; the trials of TODAY
He bears for us who walked life's toilsome way.
Christ is our Hope; the FUTURE all unknown
Is in His care who watches from the throne.

If you would master temptation, let Christ master you.

Christ is needed on the avenue as much as in the alley.

Life with Christ is an endless hope; life without Christ is a hopeless end.

Holiness is not the way to Christ, Christ is the way to holiness.

Jesus Christ is no security against storms, but He is a perfect security in storms. He has never promised you an easy passage, only a safe landing.

He that is mastered by Christ is the master of many circumstances.

It is better to be with Christ in the storm than in smooth water without Him.

Peace rules the day when Christ rules the soul.

If we want an increase of Christ, there must first be a decrease of self.

CHRIST IS THE WAY— men without Him are like Cain, wanderers and vagabonds.
CHRIST IS THE TRUTH— men without Him are liars, like the devil.
CHRIST IS THE LIGHT— men without Him walk in darkness and know not whither they go.
CHRIST IS THE LIFE— men without Him are dead in trespasses and sin.
CHRIST IS THE VINE— men who are not in Him are withered branches prepared for the fire.
CHRIST IS THE ROCK— men not built on Him are carried away by the flood of judgment.
O BLESSED CHRIST, how much better would it not to be, than to be without Thee!

Christ is not VALUED AT ALL unless He is valued ABOVE ALL.

CENTER
your Christmas
in
CHRIST

If you want to know how precious Christ can be, make Him pre-eminent.

The Son of God became the Son of Man
that he might change
the sons of men into sons of God.

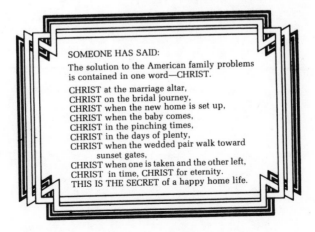

SOMEONE HAS SAID:

The solution to the American family problems is contained in one word—CHRIST.

CHRIST at the marriage altar,
CHRIST on the bridal journey,
CHRIST when the new home is set up,
CHRIST when the baby comes,
CHRIST in the pinching times,
CHRIST in the days of plenty,
CHRIST when the wedded pair walk toward
    sunset gates,
CHRIST when one is taken and the other left,
CHRIST in time, CHRIST for eternity.
THIS IS THE SECRET of a happy home life.

Christian

One with God is a majority.

Every true Christian can boast
of having three degrees;
B.A. — Born Again
M.A. — Mightily Altered
D.D. — Divinely Destined.

Scripture gives four names to Christians:
SAINTS for their holiness,
BELIEVERS for their faith,
BRETHREN for their love,
DISCIPLES for their knowledge.

The secret of being a saint
is being a saint in secret.

To return evil for good is DEVILISH:
To return good for good is HUMAN;
To return good for evil is GOD-LIKE.

The Christian's life is the world's Bible.

He who is born of God should
grow to resemble his father.

JESUS first,
YOURSELF last,
and NOTHING between
spells
J O Y
in the true sense.

A stranger is one away from home,
but a pilgrim is one who is on his way home.

A Christian is free
but not free to sin.

It is wonderful to be on the "ins" with God
and on the "outs" with nobody but the devil.
—T. J. Bach

51

Reckon him a Christian indeed who is not ashamed of the Gospel nor a shame to it.

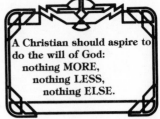
A Christian should aspire to do the will of God:
nothing MORE,
nothing LESS,
nothing ELSE.

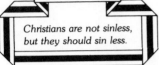
Christians are not sinless, but they should sin less.

It costs nothing to become a Christian, **but it costs everything to be a Christian.**

Only those who are truly BOUND to Christ are truly FREE.

Real Christians are forgiven, forgiving, and for giving.
Their sins are forgiven by God.
They themselves forgive those who wrong them.
And a generous spirit prompts them to give cheerfully
to the work of the Lord.

— *R. L. Cox*

FAITH *makes a man a Christian.*
His LIFE *proves he is a Christian.*
TRIAL *confirms him as a Christian*
DEATH *crowns him as a Christian.*

The Christian who claims the promises of God should obey the commands of God.

Two marks of a Christian:
GIVING
and
FORGIVING

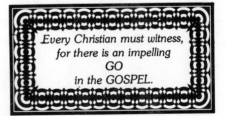
Every Christian must witness,
for there is an impelling
GO
in the GOSPEL.

Nothing can make a trusting Christian blue.

Day by day,
dear Lord,
of Thee three things I pray:
to see Thee more clearly,
to love Thee more dearly,
and to follow Thee more truly
day by day.

Five things are seen in connection with the sheep:
(1) The Believer's Relationship - "My sheep."
(2) The Believer's Privilege - "Hear My voice."
(3) The Believer's Walk - "Follow Me."
(4) The Believer's Portion - "Eternal Life."
(5) The Believer's Security - "Never Perish."

My sheep hear my voice . . . and they follow me: and I give unto them eternal life; and they shall never perish, neither shall any man pluck them out of my hand.

John 10:27, 28

A Christian is one who does not have to consult his bank book to see how wealthy he really is.

If you are a Christian, remember that men judge your Lord by you.

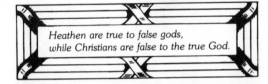

Heathen are true to false gods,
while Christians are false to the true God.

THE CHRISTIAN LIFE COMPARED TO—
An EAGLE hastening to the prey (Job 9:26)
A PILGRIMAGE (Gen. 47:9)
A TALE told (Ps. 90:9)
A SWIFT POST (Job 9:25)
A SWIFT SHIP (Job 9:26)
A HAND-BREATH (Ps. 39:5)
A SHEPHERD'S TENT removed (Isa. 38:8)
A DREAM (Ps. 73:20)
A SLEEP (Ps. 90:5)
A VAPOR (James 4:14)
A SHADOW (Eccles. 6:12)
A THREAD cut by the weaver (Isa. 38:12)
A WEAVER'S SHUTTLE (Job 7:6)
A FLOWER (Job 14:2)
GRASS (I Peter 1:24)
WATER spilled on the ground (II Sam. 14:14)
WIND (Job 7:7)

On the phrase, "IN CHRIST" hinges Paul's Epistles.
ROMANS has to do with being JUSTIFIED in Christ;
EPHESIANS, with being UNITED in Christ;
PHILIPPIANS, with being SATISFIED in Christ;
THESSALONIANS, with being GLORIFIED in Christ.

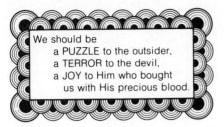

We should be
    a PUZZLE to the outsider,
    a TERROR to the devil,
    a JOY to Him who bought
        us with His precious blood.

Christians are like tea: their strength is not drawn out until they get in hot water.

*Learn to BEAR
and to FORBEAR,
FORGET
and FORGIVE;
For this is the way all
Christians should live.*

Reckon him a Christian indeed who is not ashamed of the Gospel nor a shame to it.

No man ever regretted
CHRISTIANITY
on his deathbed.

He always wins who sides with God; to Him no cause is lost.

CHRISTIAN

It is not the ship in the water but the water in the ship that sinks it. So it is not the Christian in the world but the world in the Christian that constitutes the danger.

Anything that dims my vision of Christ, or takes away my taste for Bible study, or cramps my prayer life, or makes Christian work difficult, is wrong for me, and I must, as a Christian, turn away from it.

— J. Wilbur Chapman

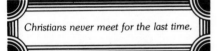

Christians never meet for the last time.

Some Christians are like the Arctic rivers—
frozen at the mouth.

Conversion may be the work of a moment, but a saint is not made overnight.

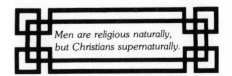

Men are religious naturally, but Christians supernaturally.

Church

Ask yourself, "What kind of a church would ours be if everyone was like I am?"

Some people devote all their religion to going to church.

A CHURCH GARDEN

Three Rows of Squash
1. Squash indifference.
2. Squash criticism.
3. Squash gossip.

Four Rows of Turnips
1. Turn up for meetings.
2. Turn up with a smile.
3. Turn up with a visitor.
4. Turn up with a Bible.

Five Rows of Lettuce
1. Let us love one another.
2. Let us welcome strangers.
3. Let us be faithful to duty.
4. Let us truly worship God.
5. Let us give liberally.

Some people are like buzzards— they never go to church unless someone dies.

What the church needs is less BLOCK and more TACKLE.

The best remedy for a sick church is to put it on a missionary diet.

SOME DON'TS FOR CHURCH ATTENDERS

Don't visit; worship.
Don't hurry away; speak and be spoken to.
Don't dodge the preacher; show yourself friendly.
Don't dodge the collection plate; contribute what you are able.
Don't sit in the end of the pew; move over.
Don't stare blankly while others sing; join in.
Don't wait for an introduction; introduce yourself.
Don't criticize; remember your own frailties.
Don't monopolize your hymn book; be neighborly.
Don't stay away from church because you have company; bring them with you.
Don't stay away from church because the church is not perfect; how lonely you would feel in a perfect church.

Some people have only three occasions for attending church: When they are hatched, matched, and dispatched.

Some churches seem to be sound in doctrine, but they are sound asleep.

You can't build a church with stumbling blocks.

Tonight, my soul, be still and sleep;
The storms are raging on God's deep—
God's deep, not thine; be still and sleep;
Tonight, my soul, be still and sleep;
God's hand shall still the tempest's sweep—
God's hand, not thine; be still and sleep.

THE COST OF CONSECRATED LIVING

It cost ABRAHAM the yielding up of his son.
It cost DANIEL to be cast in the lions' den.
It cost STEPHEN death by stoning.
It cost PETER a martyr's death.
It cost PAUL to be beheaded.
It cost JESUS to die on the cross.
DOES IT COST YOU ANYTHING?

YESTERDAY is gone forever;
TOMORROW never comes;
God places the emphasis upon the NOW of TODAY.

Commitment

George Muller's advice to those who desired to know the will of God:

1. Be slow to take new steps in the Lord's service, or in your business, or in your families. Weigh every thing well; weigh all in the light of the Holy Scriptures, and in the fear of God.

2. Seek to have no will of your own, in order to ascertain the mind of God regarding any steps you propose to take; so that you can honestly say you are willing to do the will of God, if He will only instruct you.

3. But when you have found out what the will of God is, seek for His help, and seek it earnestly, perseveringly, patiently, believingly, expectantly, and you will surely, in His own time and way obtain it.

Consistency

If you want to walk with God you must go God's way.

We have no right to sing:
"In the cross of Christ I glory"
unless we are willing to add,
"by whom the world is crucified
unto me and I unto the world."

Wash your own windows
and see how clean
your neighbor's look.

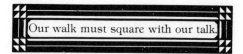

Our walk must square with our talk.

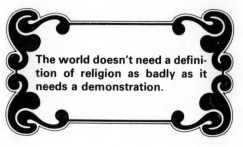

The world doesn't need a definition of religion as badly as it needs a demonstration.

It is hard to pay for bread that has been eaten.

Before you flare up at anyone's faults,
take time to count ten—
ten of your own.

A QUITTER never wins,
and a WINNER never quits.

In essentials, UNITY;
In nonessentials, LIBERTY;
In all things, LOVE.

Everywhere that Paul went,
he made some people GLAD,
some people SAD,
and some people MAD.

How seldom we weigh our neighbor in the same balance with ourselves.
—Thomas á Kempis

Let another man praise thee, and not thine own mouth, a stranger and not thine own lips (Prov. 27:2).

It is better to look ahead and prepare than to look back and regret.

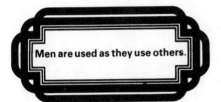

Men are used as they use others.

Remove far from me vanity and lies; give me neither poverty nor riches; feed me with food convenient for me; lest I be full, and deny thee, and say, who is the Lord? Or lest I be poor, and steal, and take the name of God in vain (Prov. 30:8-9)

Those who stand for nothing are apt to fall for anything.

So live that you wouldn't be ashamed to sell the family parrot to the town gossip.

The secret of success is consistency of purpose.

He who fears God
has nothing else to fear.

The diamond cannot be polished without friction, nor man perfected without trials.

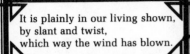
In the straight and narrow way
the traffic is all one way.

Have the grace to say,
"I was WRONG
and you were RIGHT."

It is plainly in our living shown,
by slant and twist,
which way the wind has blown.

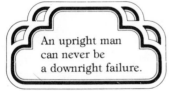
If you don't live it,
you don't believe it.

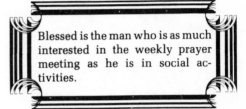
Blessed is the man who is as much
interested in the weekly prayer
meeting as he is in social ac-
tivities.

Blessed is the man whose eye-
sight will stand as much reading
in the Bible as in the Sunday
paper.

Live so your autograph will be
wanted and not your finger-
prints.

An upright man
can never be
a downright failure.

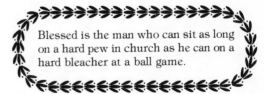
Blessed is the man who can sit as long
on a hard pew in church as he can on a
hard bleacher at a ball game.

The secret of being a saint
is being a saint in secret.

Do what you can today,
you may not be here tomorrow.

'Tis not enough to say, "I'm sorry and repent,"
And then go on from day to day just as I always went.
Repentance is to leave the sins we loved before,
And show that we in earnest grieve by doing them no more.

People look at you six days in the week
to see what you mean on the seventh.

If you want the world to heed,
put your creed
in your deed.

OUR WORDS
May hide our thoughts
BUT OUR ACTIONS
Will reveal them.

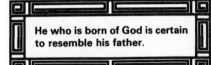
He who is born of God is certain
to resemble his father.

If a man is too busy to worship
God twice on Sunday and once on
Wednesday night, he has more
business than God intended him
to have.

J. C. Penney

A coward can praise Christ,
but it takes a man of courage
to follow Him.

A consistent Christian life is the best
interpretation and proof of the Gospel.

There is no place to hide sin
Without the conscience looking in!

The smallest good deed is better
than the grandest intention.

St. Francis of Assisi was hoeing
his garden when someone asked
what he would do if he were
suddenly to learn that he would
die before sunset. "I would finish
hoeing my garden." he replied.

69

The person who is pulling the oars usually hasn't time to rock the boat.

By the outward acts we can judge the inward thoughts.

It is more important to watch how a man lives than to listen to what he says.

Fewer people would be in debt if they didn't spend what their friends think they make.

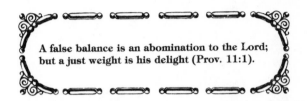

A false balance is an abomination to the Lord; but a just weight is his delight (Prov. 11:1).

The best test of a man's doctrine is the application of it in his own life.

Revenge is the sword that wounds the one who wields it.

Be an "AMEN" Christian, but don't shout it any louder than you live it.

The person who stays out of church because there are too many hypocrites in it, is doing the right thing; one more wouldn't improve the situation.

It isn't your position in life that counts— it's your disposition.

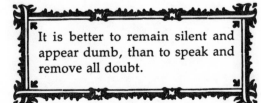

It is better to remain silent and appear dumb, than to speak and remove all doubt.

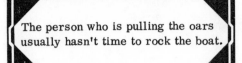

Life is like a mirror—
if you frown at it,
it frowns back;
if you smile,
it returns the greeting.

An easy conscience makes a soft pillow.

When men speak ill of you,
so live that no one will believe them.

And shall I use these ransomed powers of mine
For things that only minister to me?
Lord, take my tongue, my hands, my heart, my all,
And let me live and love and give for thee!

You will never have a friend if you seek one without faults.

You don't have to explain something you haven't said.

MONEY WILL BUY

A bed but not sleep.
Books but not brains.
Food but not appetite.
Finery but not beauty.
A house but not a home.
Medicine but not health.
Luxuries but not culture.
Amusements but not happiness.
Religion but not salvation.

The voice of a holy life often speaks loudest when the tongue is silent.

Tell me your company and I will tell you who you are.

A sound argument must have more than sound to it.

Be not angry that you cannot make others
as you wish them to be,
since you cannot make yourself
as you wish to be.
—Thomas á Kempis

Blessed is the man who can adjust
to a set of circumstances without
surrendering his convictions.

Where God's finger points,
God's hand will always make the way.

Be what your friends think you are;
avoid what your enemies say you are;
go right ahead and be happy.

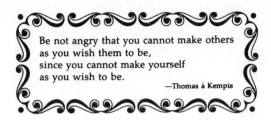

The reason a dog has so many
friends is because he wags his
tail instead of his tongue.

There are two parts to the Gospel:
believing it and behaving it.

If the Lord intended for us to
live in a permissive society,
wouldn't the Ten Command-
ments have been the Ten Sug-
gestions?

Criticism

It is easy to acquire the fault-finding habit but it is hard to be liberated from it.

When looking for faults,
use a
MIRROR
not a
TELESCOPE

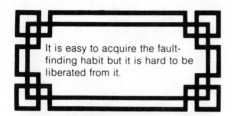

How seldom we weigh our neighbor in the same balance with ourselves.
—Thomas á Kempis

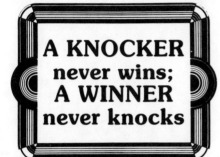

God has given us two ears, two eyes, and one tongue, to the end that we should hear and see more than we speak.

Criticism can be avoided by
saying nothing,
doing nothing,
and being nothing.

Worse than the sin you criticize is the sin of criticism.

The man who is always finding fault seldom finds anything else.

Nobody raises his own reputation by lowering others.

It is much easier to be critical than to be correct.

Nothing is easier than fault-finding:
it takes no talent,
no self-respect,
no brains,
no character,
to set up the grumbling business.

Discipline

The rod and reproof give wisdom: but a child left to himself bringeth his mother to shame (Prov. 29:15).

It is less painful to
DISCIPLINE
a child
than to
WEEP OVER
a spoiled youth.

Withhold not correction from the child: for if thou beatest him with the rod, he shall not die (Prov. 23:13).

Chasten thy son while there is hope, and let not thy soul spare for his crying (Prov. 19:18).

He who reigns within himself,
and rules passions, desires, and fears,
is more than a king.

On Sunday morning it is often a debate between ought and auto.

A good father, finding his son on the wrong track, will provide switching facilities.

Everything nowadays is controlled by switches —except children.

Egotism

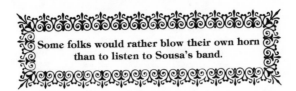

Some folks would rather blow their own horn
than to listen to Sousa's band.

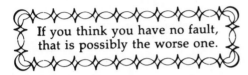

If you think you have no fault,
that is possibly the worse one.

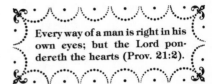

Every way of a man is right in his
own eyes; but the Lord pon-
dereth the hearts (Prov. 21:2).

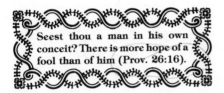

Seest thou a man in his own
conceit? There is more hope of a
fool than of him (Prov. 26:16).

No matter how stony the path,
some forge ahead; no matter how
easy the going, some lag behind.

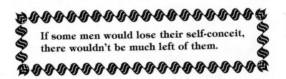

If some men would lose their self-conceit,
there wouldn't be much left of them.

One of the hardest secrets for a man
to keep
is his opinion
of himself.

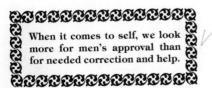

When it comes to self, we look
more for men's approval than
for needed correction and help.

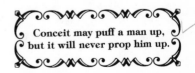

Conceit may puff a man up,
but it will never prop him up.

Faithfulness

God measures our gifts not by the greatness of them, but by the self-denial they express in giving them.

The greater danger for most of us is not that our aim is too high and we miss it, but that it is too low and we reach it.

Consider the postage stamp.
Its usefulness lies in
the ability to stick to one thing
until completed.

Count that day lost whose low descending sun views from thy hand no worthy action done.

The man who is worse than a quitter is the man who is afraid to begin.

You can do anything you want to, if you want to do what you ought to do.

There has never been a statue erected to the memory of someone who left well enough alone.

God's part we cannot do;
our part He will not do.

To get the true measure of a man's capacity, note how much more he does than is required of him.

If we are faithful, God will look after our success.

It is not success that God rewards but always the faithfulness of doing His will.

My Lord knows the way through the wilderness. All I have to do is follow.

Each morning sees some task begun,
Each evening sees its close;
Something attempted, something done
Has earned a night's repose.

—Longfellow

Have a purpose in life,
and having it,
throw into your work
such strength
of mind and muscle
as God has given you.

**Keep waiting
ON HIM
keep working
WITH HIM
keep watching
FOR HIM.**

**What you
CAN DO
you
OUGHT TO DO,
and what you
OUGHT TO DO,
by the help of God
DO!**

Be like the watch:
have an open face,
busy hands,
full of good works,
pure gold, and
well regulated.

**Depend on it—
God's work
done in
God's way,
will never lack
God's supplies.**

God

He who makes God first will find God with him at the last.

If God could speak through Balaam's ass, He surely can speak through you.

If you have God's promise for a thing, isn't that enough?

Only he who sees the invisible can do the impossible.

God chastens us with many instruments, but they are all held in His ever-loving hand.

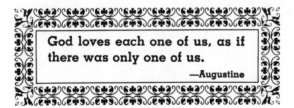

God loves each one of us, as if there was only one of us.

—Augustine

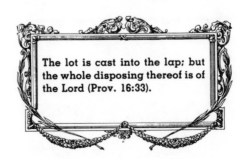

The lot is cast into the lap; but the whole disposing thereof is of the Lord (Prov. 16:33).

One of the greatest evidences of God's love to those who love Him is to send afflictions with grace to bear them.

God wants men,
   but He does not need them;
Men need God,
   but they do not want Him.

If you will be all God wants you to be, then you can do all God wants you to do.

While our heavenly Father does not promise a comfortable journey, He does guarantee a safe landing.

God never commands and commissions without providing grace to obey.

It is equally easy for God to supply our greatest as well as our smallest wants, to carry our heaviest as well as our lightest burden — just as the ocean bears the battleship as easily as it does the fisherman's vessel.

Many people believe in God, but not many believe God.

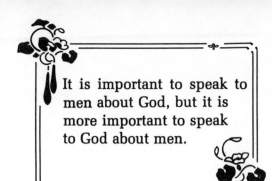

It is important to speak to men about God, but it is more important to speak to God about men.

There is nothing God will not do through one who does not care to whom the credit goes.

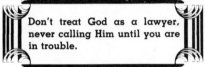

Don't treat God as a lawyer, never calling Him until you are in trouble.

God never closes one door without opening another.

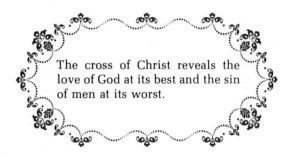

The cross of Christ reveals the love of God at its best and the sin of men at its worst.

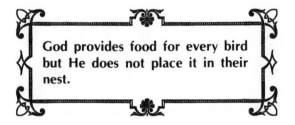

God provides food for every bird but He does not place it in their nest.

The peace of God passeth all understanding and misunderstanding.

In order to mould His people, God often has to melt them.

Home

Home is the place where we are treated best and grumble most.

A stranger is one away from home, but a pilgrim is on his way home.

A HOUSE is built of logs and stones,
Of tiles and posts and tiers;
A HOME is built of loving deeds
That stand a thousand years.

The first indication of domestic happiness is the love of one's home.

One of the most important pieces of furniture for the home is the family altar.

If your house is merely a place to eat and sleep, it ceases to be home.

A little girl, who was asked where her home was, said, "Where mother is."

A broken home is the world's greatest wreck.

A Christian home is earth's sweetest picture of heaven.

Lighter Vein

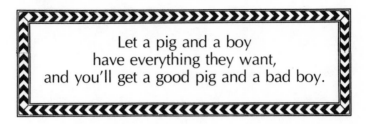

Let a pig and a boy
have everything they want,
and you'll get a good pig and a bad boy.

Some husbands know all the answers because they have been listening for years.

Distance lends enchantment, but not when you're out of gas.

A black cat following you is bad luck, depending on whether you are a man or a mouse.

Some people have only three occasions for attending church: when they are hatched, matched, and dispatched.

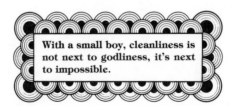

With a small boy, cleanliness is not next to godliness, it's next to impossible.

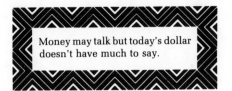

Money may talk but today's dollar doesn't have much to say.

When a man won't listen to his conscience, it's usually because he doesn't want advice from a total stranger.

You would get cheated if you gave a penny for some people's thoughts.

A lot of folks who never took music lessons are good at fiddling around.

Some folks would rather blow their own horn than listen to Sousa's band.

Face powder may catch a man, but it takes baking powder to hold him.

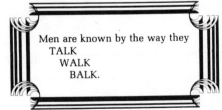

Men are known by the way they
    TALK
      WALK
        BALK.

CHEER UP! Birds also have bills, but they keep on singing.

Love

If slighted, slight the slight, and love the slighter.

Charity (love) begins at home — but it does not stay there.

*Love sent my Lord
to the cross of shame,
Love found a way,
O praise His holy name!*

Law makes us act from outward compulsion, but love makes us serve from inward compassion.

It is never loving that empties the heart, nor giving that empties the purse.

Better a dinner of herbs where love is, than a stalled ox and hatred thereby (Prov. 15:17).

"Tis better to have loved and lost
Than never to have loved at all.

— Tennyson

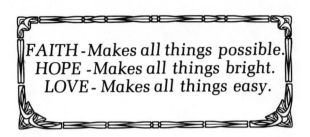

FAITH -Makes all things possible.
HOPE -Makes all things bright.
LOVE - Makes all things easy.

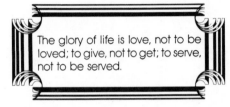

The glory of life is love, not to be loved; to give, not to get; to serve, not to be served.

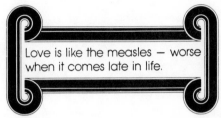

Love is like the measles — worse when it comes late in life.

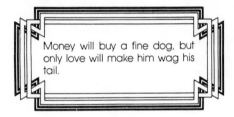

Money will buy a fine dog, but only love will make him wag his tail.

Love looks through a telescope; envy through a microscope.

The sunlight of love will kill all the germs of jealousy and hate.

A "bit of love" is the only bit that will put a bridle on the tongue.
— Beck

Love is its own reward;
hate is its own punishment.

It is natural to love them that love us,
but it is supernatural to love them that hate us.

Duty makes us do things well,
but love makes us do them beautifully.

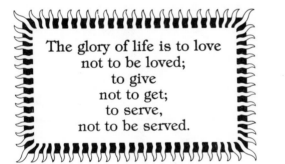
The glory of life is to love
not to be loved;
to give
not to get;
to serve,
not to be served.

Works, and not
words, are the
proof of love.

There is more pleasure in loving
than in being loved.

Prayer

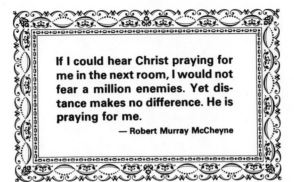

If I could hear Christ praying for me in the next room, I would not fear a million enemies. Yet distance makes no difference. He is praying for me.

— Robert Murray McCheyne

More things are wrought by prayer than the world dreams of.

Arguments never settle things, but prayer changes things.

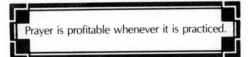

Prayer is profitable whenever it is practiced.

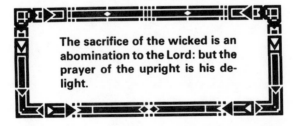

The sacrifice of the wicked is an abomination to the Lord: but the prayer of the upright is his delight.

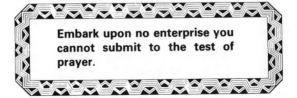

Embark upon no enterprise you cannot submit to the test of prayer.

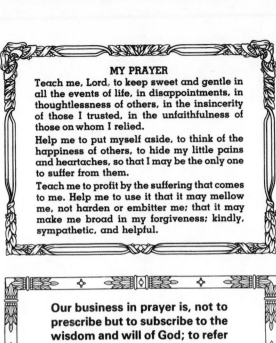

MY PRAYER

Teach me, Lord, to keep sweet and gentle in all the events of life, in disappointments, in thoughtlessness of others, in the insincerity of those I trusted, in the unfaithfulness of those on whom I relied.

Help me to put myself aside, to think of the happiness of others, to hide my little pains and heartaches, so that I may be the only one to suffer from them.

Teach me to profit by the suffering that comes to me. Help me to use it that it may mellow me, not harden or embitter me; that it may make me broad in my forgiveness; kindly, sympathetic, and helpful.

Our business in prayer is, not to prescribe but to subscribe to the wisdom and will of God; to refer our case to Him, and then leave it with Him.

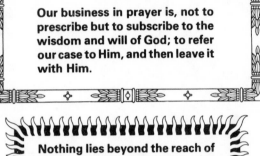

Nothing lies beyond the reach of prayer except that which lies beyond the will of God.

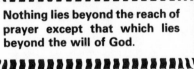

He stands best who kneels most.

Without prayer no work is well done.

Daily prayers lessen daily cares.

Prayerless pews make powerless pulpits.

Prayer is hardest when it is hardest to pray.

God's answers are wiser than our prayers.

Change matters of care to matters of prayer.

Do not face the day until you have faced God.

Unanswered yet! Nay, do not say UNGRANTED;
perhaps your part is not yet fully done.
The work began when first your prayer was uttered,
and God will finish what He has begun.
If you keep faith's incense burning there,
His glory you will see—sometime—somewhere!

Service

The believer's talents are not to be
laid up for self
but laid out in service.

No matter how small your lot may
be in life, there is always room
for a service station.

Service was never intended
as a substitute
for a godly life.

We are saved to serve,
but we never serve to get saved.

Hard work, cheerfully done,
is easy work.
Light work, unwillingly done,
is mere drudgery.

True service is love for Christ
in working clothes.

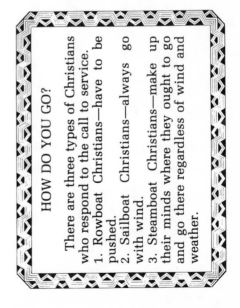

HOW DO YOU GO?

There are three types of Christians
who respond to the call to service.
1. Rowboat Christians—have to be
pushed.
2. Sailboat Christians—always go
with wind.
3. Steamboat Christians—make up
their minds where they ought to go
and go there regardless of wind and
weather.

Sin

The backslider runs from the Lord when he walks in his own way.

Lying and stealing live next door to each other.

You hate sin just insofar as you love Christ.

Sin may come upon thee by surprise, but do not let it dwell with thee as a guest.

Sin has many tools, but a lie is a handle that fits them all.

Sin is its own detective.

Few love to hear of the sins they love to act.

Sin causes the Christian's cup of joy to spring a leak.

Warning

The measure of a man's real character is what he would do if he knew he would never be found out.

He that being often reproved hardeneth his neck, shall suddenly be destroyed, and that without remedy (Prov. 29:1).

To every man opens a high way and a low way and every man decides the way that he shall go.

What you laugh at tells plainer than words what you are.

If you are not as close to God as you once were, you need not wonder who it is who moved.

It is easy to give another a piece of your mind, but when you are through, you may have lost your peace of mind.

Beware, Christian, of three things: doubt, dirt, and debt.

A man's reputation is only what men think him to be; his character is what God knows him to be.

The pleasures of sin are for a season; but its wages are eternal.

Whoso stoppeth his ears at the cry of the poor, he also shall cry himself but shall never be heard (Prov. 12:13).

The best way to wipe out a friendship is to sponge on it.

He who cannot forgive others breaks the bridge over which he himself must pass.

The real problem of your leisure is how to keep other people from using it.

Wisdom

We learn wisdom from failure much more than from success.

Only one life,
'twill soon be past,
only what's done for Christ
will last.

He is no fool
who parts with that
he cannot keep,
to get that
which he shall
not lose.

Forethought
is better than
repentance.

The fruit of the righteous is a tree of life; and he that winneth souls is wise (Prov. 11:30).

He that is slow to wrath is of great understanding; but he that is hasty in spirit exalteth folly (Prov. 14:19).

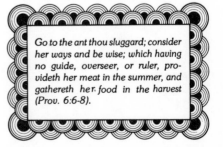

Go to the ant thou sluggard; consider her ways and be wise; which having no guide, overseer, or ruler, provideth her meat in the summer, and gathereth her food in the harvest (Prov. 6:6-8).

119

Worldliness

With such a starting point as the cross and such a goal as the Lord's coming, how can a Christian love the things of the world, the flesh, and the devil?

The wise men of Jesus' day presented frankincense. The worldly wise of our day present rank nonsense.

The more we are transformed by the power of Christ, the less we will be conformed to this world.

Chasing after pleasure is a confession of an unsatisfied life.

You can't "wait on the Lord" and "run with the devil" at the same time.

The more of heaven there is in our lives, the less of earth we shall covet.

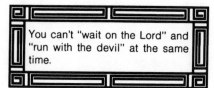

Lie down with dogs and you'll get up with fleas.

The path of the world seems pleasant enough if you don't stop to think where you're going.

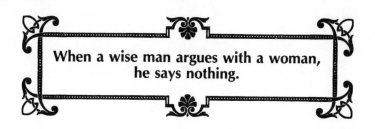
When a wise man argues with a woman,
he says nothing.

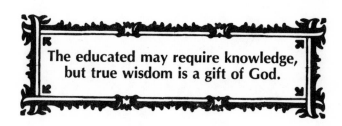
The educated may require knowledge,
but true wisdom is a gift of God.

He who shall introduce into public affairs the
principles of primitive Christianity,
will revolutionize the world.
— Benjamin Franklin

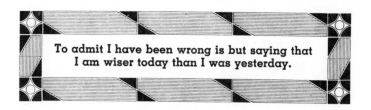
To admit I have been wrong is but saying that
I am wiser today than I was yesterday.

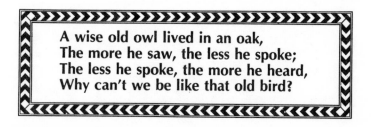
A wise old owl lived in an oak,
The more he saw, the less he spoke;
The less he spoke, the more he heard,
Why can't we be like that old bird?

Worry

Worry is like a rocking chair;
it will give you something to do
but it won't get you anywhere.

Nothing can make
a trusting Christian blue.

Fear and faith cannot keep house together
When one enters, the other departs.

Why worry when
you can pray?

Fear is unbelief
parading in disguise.

It is only the fear of God
that can deliver us
from the fear of men.

The eagle that soars near the sun
is not concerned
how it will cross the raging stream.

Dr. Charles Mayo said: "I've never known a man who died of hard work, but many who die of worry."

If your all is in the hand of the Lord, why worry about what "they say"?

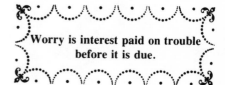

Worry is interest paid on trouble before it is due.

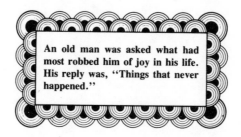

An old man was asked what had most robbed him of joy in his life. His reply was, "Things that never happened."